The
UPSIDES
TO DOWNSIZING

Housing Options for Easy Living

JACKIE WHITE

ILLUMIFY
MEDIA.COM

The Upsides to Downsizing

Published by
Illumify Media Global
www.IllumifyMedia.com
"Let's bring your book to life!"

Paperback ISBN: 978-1-959099-71-0

Cover design by Debbie Lewis

Printed in the United States of America

CONTENTS

INTRODUCTION

"There's no place like home."
— Dorothy Gale, *The Wizard of Oz*

There really is no place like your home. It's where you raise your family. Celebrate milestones. And find comfort and solace. It's your legacy—the culmination of all you've worked for.

Your home quite literally houses your memories. It's a reflection of you, your children, grandchildren, family dinners, memorable moments, friends, birthdays, anniversaries, and so much more.

No wonder people are so emotionally tied to their homes.

As an established Realtor selling homes in the Denver area and front range foothills west of Denver, I have sold nearly three hundred homes in the past ten years. Many of my clients are empty nesters or retirees. Perhaps like you, they have lived in their homes for many years—sometimes decades—and are ready for a lifestyle that favors simplicity, convenience, and maintenance-free living.

Or perhaps they have health issues that require easier, one-level living closer to their health care providers. Sometimes their house is just too much to handle, and the cost of maintenance is no longer an option.

But downsizing doesn't have to be overwhelming. In fact, there are many upsides to it! So how do you know where to start?

The good news: you don't have to be a wizard to know how to navigate the process. You just need this guide and a professional Realtor you trust.

So, click your heels three times and keep reading to find out what the upsides to downsizing are … and how it can be one of the best decisions of your life.

ONE

MAKING THE MOVE

ARE YOU READY?

Maria and Sam were newlyweds when they bought their first home twenty-five years ago. It was nestled in the foothills of Colorado, offered easy access to hiking and skiing—and great schools for their two kids.

As the years passed, the couple still enjoyed skiing, but Maria took a tumble on the slopes and had knee surgery. It left her nervous about the steep terrain. At the same time, Sam picked up tennis, and the league he played in was in town—a thirty-minute drive away. Their oldest child left for college and their youngest adult son was still living at home.

Maria and Sam came to a decision: It was time

to sell their home. It provided exactly what they needed at the time they needed it twenty-five years ago. But now, there were many reasons to downsize.

They sold their home and moved into a more convenient townhome closer to their new activities and friends. Their youngest son finally moved out and was able to take some of the extra furniture from the home he grew up in for his new apartment!

∽

You probably know a family like Maria and Sam's. Or maybe it sounds like your situation. When you purchase a home in which to raise your family, you aren't thinking about twenty-five, thirty-five, or fifty years later. You're thinking of what you need and can afford at the time.

But time and life catch up—and what you needed then isn't what you may need (or can afford) now.

Is it easier to stay exactly where you are? Sure. But your circumstances might say otherwise. Many empty nesters, retirees, and seniors who are in a new chapter of their lives face the following:

- Burdensome costs of maintaining their homes.
- A major life event, such as a health issue.
- The need and desire to be closer to adult children and grandchildren.
- Financial concerns that require a different lifestyle.
- Simply not needing all that space anymore.

Whatever your reason, selling a home is one of the biggest decisions of your life—right up there with getting married, taking a job, and having children. And like *those* life situations, selling a home has many practical, financial, and emotional implications.

So how do you know if you're ready?

Preparing Emotionally

Many of us are attached to our homes. You've poured sweat equity, time, and money into making it your own. You've raised children and created memories there. You know every nook and cranny. You remember your kids' sleepovers there. You know the small hole in the hallway that is now covered by a framed photo.

It's natural to feel emotionally connected to our home. And it's equally important to remember that those loving memories will never go away.

Moving—and moving on—is a process. As you

prepare your home to go on the market, you have to prepare yourself too.

So how do you start? Remember, selling your home is a business transaction. Don't make the mistake of letting your emotions hold you back from something that will benefit you and your family now and into the future.

Here are three ways to help you prepare emotionally:

1. Write down a list of reasons why you want to move. Keep the list handy to remind yourself of what you'll gain (not lose) by selling your home. Put it on your fridge or somewhere visible, so you'll see each day.

2. Find the right Realtor. If they're worth their salt, they will know where the emotional landmines are and can help you navigate them. It's important to be honest about your concerns. Your real estate professional wants the best outcome for you. Resisting their suggestions or not being honest with yourself about wanting to sell or move will only hinder the process. Consider seeking the guidance of a Senior Real Estate Specialist. Realtors earn this special designation through countless hours of continuing education and are uniquely

qualified to understand the needs of seniors during a home sale or purchase.

3. Start thinking of your home as a product on the market. You'll have to organize, declutter, and clean—perhaps even paint and polish—your home to be ready for buyers. When you hear critical feedback from potential buyers, don't fall into the trap of reacting emotionally. You are selling property for purchase. You won't be living there anymore—someone else will. The sooner you acknowledge that, the easier the process of detaching will become.

In the end, if you're unable to loosen the heart-strings on your home, wait a while before you consider selling. Pull out that list of reasons why selling is beneficial to you and keep marching forward toward new memories.

Getting on the Same Page

Let's face it. You may think you know exactly where your partner or spouse stands on an issue. But until you discuss it openly and honestly—and in detail—you never *really* know.

Sometimes, we say things our partner wants to hear because it's the path of least resistance. One way to see if you're on the same page is to have your partner make a list of pros and cons of selling your home. Make one yourself and then compare them. This will let you know whether you're in lockstep about the decision to sell and the steps involved in preparing.

Next, discuss some of the upcoming details. It's one thing to "say" you're on the same page and share the same vision. It's quite another to start working together through the many complex details ahead.

PRO TIP: Before agreeing to put your home on the market, walk through some of the big issues you must consider when selling a home. If you can say yes to the questions below, you're probably on the same page and ready to sell.

- Do you both understand the current market conditions?
- Do you both know your property's value and agree on a listing price?
- Do you agree on what to do with your home's equity?
- Are you both financially prepared to move (and buy)?
- Do you know where you want to move— location, type of home, and price range?
- Is the timing right for both of you?

Understanding Taxes!

Most people know you must pay property taxes on your home. But are you also aware that selling your home can trigger significant tax consequences?

That's right. You may owe Uncle Sam a lot of money in capital gains taxes just for the privilege of selling your own home. But there are ways to stay ahead of this pesky tax. The key is being prepared!

Capital gains taxes usually apply in situations where the proceeds from the sale of your home aren't used to buy another home. The "gain" is the difference between the selling price and the purchase price.

The tax rate you pay is based on many factors, such as how long you held onto your property. It is important to consult with your accountant or financial advisor to understand this specific topic. If you don't have an accountant or financial advisor, you should find one. Your real estate agent should have a network of professionals for you. If they don't or give you a blank stare when you ask about capital gains taxes, look for a real estate agent who does.

And fast!

Understanding Legal Forms!

It's hard to think of our kids as adults sometimes. But if your kids are older, then they should be able to partici-pate in the sale of your home and help you prepare for it.

If you've already begun working with a real estate agent, make sure you designate yourself or someone in your family as the lead contact. Having too many voices communicating with your real estate agent can slow the process down and make it disorganized.

If you or your partner are ill or worried about becoming incapacitated, you should consider giving one of your children or trusted family member or friend power of attorney to make legally binding decisions about the home on your behalf.

As with taxes, always consult a legal professional about your specific situation.

Telling Your Family

Remember Maria and Sam, the couple at the beginning of this chapter?

One of their children was away at college when they sold their home. But the other adult child was still living at home.

Just as you might have an emotional attachment to your home, so will your family and kids. It's important to have open discussions about why you are considering selling, what the next chapter looks like, and where they fit in. Allow them to be a part of the many decisions in the weeks and months ahead. Lean on them to help you declutter and organize. Make them a part of the process.

And like Maria and Sam's son, maybe they'll even get some furniture out of the deal.

Most of all, acknowledge the many memories the home held for you as a family and reassure them that new memories are always being made.

Because home isn't simply a house. It's wherever your family is.

Selling your home is a significant event in your life —especially for empty nesters and seniors. Make sure you're emotionally and financially ready. Speak openly with your partner and your family. And get professional advice, starting with an experienced Realtor, preferably a Senior Real Estate Specialist, who knows your market and understands your situation.

So, are you ready to sell?

Are you ready to move?

Are you ready for the next chapter of this book— and your life?

Read on!

TWO
FINDING A HOME THAT FITS YOUR NEEDS

Steve and Paula were living in a ranch-style home and enjoying their Colorado mountain views. But the location was a little remote for their more frequent doctor appointments and errands.

After the birth of their first grandchild, they found themselves traveling to Minneapolis to see their grandchildren pretty frequently. Purchasing a new townhome with an HOA a little closer to town and the airport would allow them to "lock and leave," so they could visit family for weeks at a time without having to worry about maintenance.

While the builder was finishing the home, Steve and Paula decided to have an elevator installed. They were in good health at the time, but they were thinking the future might make the stairs a little more challenging. With an elevator, they were already planning on how to grow older in a new home they love.

～

There's an emerging trend for baby boomers. Traditional senior care facilities are no longer the only option. In fact, retiring doesn't mean heading for a home where pudding and peas are daily menu items. We're living longer and aging in place, prioritizing wellness through affordability, lifestyle, and autonomy. Boomers value socialization and community.

Finding a home that supports your lifestyle during your golden years is key.

It's golden because that shiny new home you're considering downsizing to is finally in your sights. And though it might not seem like work to imagine exactly the home with precisely the bells and whistles you want, it really is work.

For starters, there's the matter of figuring out which type of home fits your budget and lifestyle. Scroll through a real estate website and you'll see a range of properties from modern and minimalist to rustic and expansive. Where to begin?

Let's put it a different way: If *you* were a house, what kind of house would you be? To answer, let's look at your lifestyle.

If you're a reader, maybe you want a library in your home. If you're a cooking enthusiast, you'll want a gourmet kitchen. Or maybe a few decades ago, you were so busy raising children and working that you didn't get to truly spend time doing what you loved, such as gardening.

But now?

Cue game show host voice …

"Grab the trowel and dirt—because you're going to get cozy with the tulips in your brand … new … one-level ranch home on two garden-ready acres!"

So, what kind of lifestyle do you have? Here are a few of the more common ones for those of us who have reached a stage in life where we're ready to focus on what fulfills us.

The Traveler

Many people who approach midlife and beyond start to think about traveling more. Sailing the seas. Flying the friendly skies. Visiting the vistas—because they just didn't have the time or financial stability to do so earlier.

Or perhaps you have kids and grandkids in different parts of the country and plan to visit fairly frequently. If so, this is a chapter of your life where you'll no doubt rack up mileage points, keep a favorite suitcase handy, and discover your own tricks and tips to traveling made easy.

And *easy* is the name of the game when it comes to finding a home that matches a traveler's lifestyle. There are generally three types of lifestyles that fall under this category:

1. Snowbirds. Those in search of warmer weather. It's nearly a rite of passage to have a second home in a warmer climate for the winter. As we get older, our tolerance for the cold wanes—as does our desire to deal with the hassle of snow and ice. Fortunately, there are many types of homes for snowbirds, including:

- Townhomes and condominiums
- Apartments
- Small vacation-style homes
- Timeshares
- Short-term rentals, usually found on such sites as Airbnb and Vrbo

2. Time splitters. No, this doesn't have to do with quantum physics. It's for those who split their time between cities, whether for work, family, or both. Many situations can create time splitters when it comes to places to call home. Being able to float between cities often means having homes that do not require continuous upkeep. Many people whose lifestyles fall under this category look to take advantage of maintenance-free homes—condos or townhomes with home-owner associations (HOA). The cost of an HOA is often less than paying individually for landscaping, maintenance, etc.

3. Lock and leave—these are properties for those who might leave their home unattended for longer periods of time due to extended travel or absences. Therefore, these properties often are equipped with security systems, have programmable thermostats and smart technology that you can control remotely, are in gated communities, and have secure storage.

Social Butterfly

One of the surest ways to have a long and fulfilling life is to surround yourself with friends and family. In fact, research shows that people with social connections have a higher quality of life—and can even extend their lives.

Being social and having friends leads to lower stress, better mental health, and healthier lifestyles. What's not to love?

If you're in the stage of life where you entertain and spend a majority of your time with friends, you'll want to consider the layout and space of your next home:

- Does it have a sizable kitchen where you can cook and gather?
- Is there plenty of indoor space for entertaining?
- Think about the number of guest bedrooms and bathrooms you may need.
- Don't forget about the outdoor space for everything from backyard barbecues to cocktail parties.

But what if you love your friends and being connected to social activities but don't love planning and entertaining?

There are many active adult communities with private homes just for you! You can take advantage of planned social activities to make new acquaintances, build relationships, and have a schedule full of activities with amenities including:

- Pickleball and tennis courts
- Fitness rooms
- Walking and biking trails
- Pools and clubhouses
- Golf courses
- Community centers

Happy Hobbyists

We work hard to play hard, and if you're fortunate enough to get to a stage in your life when you can spend more time on *you*, then you might be a happy hobbyist.

Whether you're easing back on work or retired, more time means you can focus on doing the things you love, whether that's woodworking, painting, yoga, crafts, or something else. But you'll need a space in your home for these passionate pursuits, such as a sewing room with space to work and storing your fabrics. A studio for your artwork or yoga. A shop or garage for your woodworking or for fixing up cars. Or maybe you are into touring the country in an RV, boating, or camping. Is there space at your home to park your recreational vehicles?

There are also other factors to consider when it comes to your hobby, such as convenience to certain stores, proper lighting, outdoor space, and so much more.

For hobbyists, be sure to check with a seasoned Realtor who is experienced in uncovering your wants and needs, understands what you like to spend your time doing, and can help match you with a home that fits your lifestyle and hobbies.

Continual Workers

Some of us either aren't ready to retire for financial reasons or love what we do so much that we want to keep working. Whatever the reason, there are more and more people who continue to have one foot in the working world no matter their age.

In this case, location may be important. You may want to be near job opportunities—which might only exist in certain markets. And if you're fortunate enough to work from home, you will need a dedicated work-space or home office. If you do, make sure to review this list of what to look for in your next home office:

- Quiet location away from busy streets or noise.
- Space that accommodates your desk, chair, equipment, and storage.
- Natural light to enhance your mood while you work.
- Reliable internet.
- Privacy for work calls or meetings.
- Temperature control, especially if you use a lot of equipment.
- Flexibility to turn the space into something for a different purpose once you stop working.

- An aesthetically pleasing space so you'll want to continue to go to work each day!

What home fits you?

First, you need to define what you love most. Because having a home that reflects you will give you a sense of purpose, passion, and fulfillment.

And who doesn't deserve that after all these years?

So, think about your interests, the stage of life you're in and where you'll be, and consider the possibilities of a home that's as much a fit for you as you are for it!

THREE
MOVING BACK IN WITH FAMILY

Larry had served as a police officer for decades and his wife, June, as a nurse in a local hospital. They were close to retirement and excited to spend more time with their new grandchildren. Larry and June's daughter and son-in-law had a toddler with another one on the way, and the cost of daycare was making their budget tight to buy a home they had their eye on to accommodate a growing family.

Larry and June decided to purchase a new construction duplex patio home right next door to their daughter and her husband. This would allow Larry and June to be available to help with childcare while giving everyone the privacy of their own separate living spaces. The sale of Larry and June's larger home gave them the ability to purchase their new home with cash, set some money aside to enjoy retirement, and help their daughter and her husband with the down payment of their new home. They now can help each other with ease, which would not have been possible if they had lived a long drive across town from one another. The grandkids are a few years older now, and they help Larry with chores around the house, like raking leaves and mowing the lawn, and are rewarded with some of June's famous chocolate chip cookies for a job well done.

〜

You've worked hard. You've raised a family. You've made a home. But now it's time to move into a new phase of your life for financial or health reasons. Or maybe you just want to press the redo button and start fresh.

Think your only option is retirement or a senior care community?

Think again.

Just as many adult children are moving in with their parents because the costs to rent or buy don't make sense for them, many parents are moving in with their adult children for the same reasons.

But there's more.

Multigenerational living is an increasing trend. The reasons aren't just financial. Sharing a living space and the responsibilities that come with that promotes bonding as well as saves money.

And isn't family everything?

If you're considering purchasing a home where you and your adult children (and grandchildren) live in the same space, there are some specific things to keep in mind to help make it a smooth transition for everyone.

Finding the Right Space

How many people in total will be living in the same space? What about entertaining guests? Will the space fit your lifestyle and theirs?

These are just a few of the questions you need to consider when everyone lives under one roof because you don't want a space that feels temporary. You want a place that feels like home for everyone and supports all lifestyles. Consider, for example:

- *Accommodating guests.* The joys of spending time with family and friends becomes less joyful if the space is cramped and someone is sleeping on the couch. The right space for you may mean extra bedrooms or a separate area for guests with their own bathroom. Make sure you talk openly with your family about the expectations for guest arrangements in your shared space.

- *Grandparents on duty!* Is there anything more wonderful than watching your grandchildren grow with the wisdom you have to impart? It's exciting to live with your grandchildren and be a critical part of their care. But if you're on full daycare duty, make sure the things you and they need— an extra bedroom for sleepovers, a playroom, a backyard, a nearby playground, a swing set—are in place. These are all things you'll need in your space to keep a young one occupied. Plan for it!

- *Are you under the same roof?* Multigenerational living isn't just one family in the same structure. There are options, especially if you're buying or purchasing a home to remodel. One possibility is a duplex—where you have your separate space and privacy but are still right next door. Many homes have a separate in-law suite where you can have your own private space within the home to keep a level of independence. And some properties include a guesthouse, or you can build one, as a completely separate structure on the same lot.

Being on the Same Page

One of the most important things you can do when considering living in a multigenerational home is to have a clear understanding of the rules and boundaries. When you raised your children, *you* were in charge. But now your children are adults. It's important to have open dialogue about expectations, including:

- *Privacy.* Everyone needs privacy, and everyone's need for privacy differs. Discuss how private spaces will be shared and respected. Make your boundaries clear.
- *Household chores.* It's easy to fall into old patterns. Maybe you were used to doing the dishes or cleaning the counters in your own home. What's the expectation when you all live together? It's critical to be clear. Everyone should be contributing to maintaining the household. But make sure you are defining exactly what that looks like and who is responsible for what.
- *Financial contributions.* Family is everything, but money can be a real sticking point. Transparency is so important to establish how the costs will be covered for housing, maintenance, food, and utilities. Everyone should ultimately

feel a sense of fairness when the specifics are clearly articulated.

- *Expectations and goals.* What do you hope living in this situation will accomplish? Aim for balance by considering everyone's hopes and goals. This is a new chapter for your family and giving everyone a chance to talk about what they hope comes from it will help you see a clear path forward.

PRO TIP #1: Consider establishing a curfew or quiet hours in the home you may be sharing. Having a designated "quiet time" where everyone is honoring a common goal can be unifying—not to mention give everyone clear boundaries.

PRO TIP #2: Keep the lines of communication open. If they close, open them again. Regular check-ins are essential. You would do the same for your car. Why not your own family? Every few months, make sure you're all still tracking toward the same goals and correct the course if you need to. An open mind, open dialogue, and a willingness to compromise are key. It's not easy living with other people—even if they're your own family. Be willing to hear what's working and what isn't to build a strong foundation of trust and respect.

Don't Miss the Exit

No good plan exists without thinking through the what ifs. Since circumstances can change, it's almost irresponsible not to plan. Your situation might suddenly look different and living with your extended family may no longer be an option. Likewise, your adult children may need to reconsider the living situation based on something that happens in *their* lives.

When this happens, be prepared with an exit strategy. Don't consider it an escape route. Consider it as solid planning for the future. And with how quickly life can change for anyone, it's a good idea to talk about it now.

First, define with your family what circumstances would necessitate a decision to move out. It could be due to health, finances, or simply wanting more solitude. Maybe living with family didn't work out as you hoped. Talk about these different scenarios and plan for them.

Next, make sure you've consulted with legal and financial advisors about issues like inheritance and property transfers. Have your bases covered now. It will be one less worry later.

Finally, know where you'll go. If you move out, will you look for a retirement community? Will you stay in the same town or state?

Plan for the Future

When it comes to multigenerational living, there's no one-size-fits-all approach. But when it works, it can be a wonderful way to promote family bonding and build more memories together. If multigenerational living is an option you are considering, keep in mind the ten must-haves below.

10 Must-Haves for Multigenerational Living:

1. The right space
2. Defined grandparents' roles (such as if daycare is expected)
3. Defined private spaces vs. shared spaces
4. An outline of household duties and expectations
5. Agreed-upon financial contributions
6. Clearly presented hopes and goals
7. Established quiet hours
8. Agreement to check in regularly with each other
9. A willingness to adjust
10. An exit plan

FOUR
SAY ADU NOT ADIEU

Mona and Gary's son and daughter-in-law moved to Colorado. When they gave birth to their first child, Mona and Gary mulled over the idea of leaving New Jersey and heading west to be with them. But Mona wasn't ready to relocate permanently. Her mother was aging, and Mona helped with her care. So the couple decided to make an investment in their future and their family by buying a condo out west and keeping their home out east.

Because they would be splitting their time between Colorado and New Jersey, they decided to rent the condo out when they weren't there and found the perfect tenants: visiting nurses who worked twelve-hour shifts and only needed a place to sleep and eat. Therefore, their condo required very little upkeep.

Mona and Gary earned rental income which helped them cover the costs of owning a second home. And when they did spend time in their condo, it allowed them to explore Denver and decide on what community would be best for them for when they would be ready to relocate permanently.

~

It sure doesn't seem like Mona and Gary downsized when they bought a second home. But they were laying the groundwork for their future downsizing by identifying an income source that provided them options.

Getting ready to downsize doesn't always mean moving from one place to another. Or even moving from where you currently live.

Perhaps you are retired and now on a fixed income. Or maybe inflation is making your house unaffordable to maintain. This is a reality for millions of American homeowners. The house you enjoyed and could once afford is now a leaky bucket of costs that are preventing you from enjoying your life and giving you a reputation as a professional coupon clipper at the local grocery store.

But you do have options beyond selling and moving (and coupon clipping).

Consider the ADU (Accessory Dwelling Unit)

Don't let the acronym scare you. It's otherwise known as an in-law suite or a granny flat. An ADU is a specific, independent living space with a bedroom, kitchen, and bathroom within or attached to a home. Many ADUs are detached but still on the property—such as a guesthouse.

ADUs are becoming more popular as costs rise, because they provide a more affordable way for seniors to live and offer passive income to property owners. There are two important things to ask yourself when mulling over an ADU.

1. Would you live in the ADU?
2. Would you own the ADU and rent it out?

You might consider living in an ADU if you're interested in:

- Maintaining your independence
- Having additional flexibility
- Staying in the neighborhood you love
- Reducing costs (more money in your pocket)

If you live in an ADU in your own neighborhood, you will likely enjoy the independence it offers in the location you love. You don't have a large house to pay for and maintain, and many ADUs are very cost-effective. They are a terrific option to consider if your house is too large and expensive, but you aren't ready for more formal senior living options.

Renting Out an ADU

An ADU just might be the solution for you if you don't want to leave your home or neighborhood but *do* want to add to your income.

If you think renting out an ADU is right for you, first do your homework to find out if ADUs are allowed where you live and what it will cost you. Consider the requirements and regulations of constructing one or converting existing space. You can visit your city's planning and zoning website as a first step. If it's too complicated to determine on your own, email city officials and ask for a meeting to explain your housing intentions. See how your goals can work within the zoning regulations or if city officials will grant permission and bend the rules through a variance.

If your community allows it, the next step is to consider the costs.

Let's say you want to convert your walkout basement into an independent living space for a family member or a tenant. The costs alone could be too high to move forward. But if you have the means and are willing to invest, you will then want to know how long it will take for the costs to be recouped before you realize income from your ADU.

Are those costs going to pay for themselves in one year? Ten years? How long are you willing to wait? Is this an investment or a lifestyle change?

PRO TIP: Create a list of some of the more common costs to consider, such as permits, construction or renovation, an increase in utilities, and the inevitable increase in annual property taxes. Next, calculate how much you would charge for rent. Then calculate how long rental income would take to pay back your investment costs.

Total investment

÷

rental income per month

=

number of months to recoup your costs

Privacy, Please

If you aren't the one living in an ADU, you need to think about how having a tenant or family member on your property can change your level of privacy.

If you love walking around in your favorite green

bathrobe, blasting music, and eating cereal at two in the morning because ... well, because you can, think about how that might go over if you have someone else in your home. Maybe they love green bathrobes too. Otherwise, consider the following:

Privacy vs. company: If you're a private person, an ADU might make you feel like your space is being encroached upon unless you set strict boundaries. On the other hand, if you like being social, perhaps a renter or family member—like your adult child or a caregiver—might be an enhancement to your lifestyle.

Barter for the space: If you have special needs, you could double up on the benefits of an ADU by allowing someone to move in who can help assist you, perhaps with chores around the house or looking after the home while you travel. In return, you might offer reduced rent or allow them to trade their services for rent.

Aging in place: Let's say your home is too large and you can no longer afford it or move around in it comfortably. You might consider staying in your own ADU on the property and selling or renting your primary residence.

Benefits of an ADU

The benefits of an ADU are more than financial. They provide a level of comfort. For those living in an ADU, the unit will provide more independence than a senior living community and are ideal for those who aren't ready for assisted living. And the emotional costs are usually substantially less than moving to a new community you may not be familiar with.

There are also typically no lawn care or maintenance costs since the homeowner will cover those. And many ADUs can be constructed for easy living with minimal stairs, for example.

They are terrific for caregivers, who might benefit from having their loved ones close.

So, is an ADU a viable way to downsize?

Yes!

You can benefit from building an ADU and earning passive income to help maintain your current home. Or you can move into an ADU to enjoy affordable convenience—proximity to family and caregivers —without losing your independence.

ADUs are quickly becoming a popular option because they are cheaper than an apartment or smaller home and easier to take care of. But they do have limits, so carefully consider what you need and what you're comfortable with.

If this option feels right for you, contact a real estate professional and request to talk about an ADU ASAP!

FIVE
PACK YOUR BAGS!

David traveled for sales, and Colorado was part of his territory. He found the community where he and Linda lived for nineteen years while on a business trip. David came across a beautiful home with views of land that would eventually become a state park. He convinced Linda to buy it sight unseen, and they enjoyed watching the thunderstorms and colorful sunsets from their home high up in the mountains for years.

As David continued to travel for work, the weather became less magical as shoveling the driveway of snow to make his early morning business flights required more effort. Their children in Ohio started having kids of their own, and it was gnawing on them that they were missing cheering for their six grandkids at Little League games and school performances. Not quite ready to retire, David was able to get a job transfer back to Ohio where he had a local territory that allowed him to be home more for family activities, and a beautiful property with flat terrain and a large barn to store his plow truck for the occasional snowstorm. No more shoveling!

~

E very phase of life requires adjustments and compromise, and downsizing is no different. As we've discussed in the prior chapters, people downsize for lots of different reasons. And thankfully, there are plenty of options that are right for you.

Sometimes, moving out of state is one of the options. The motivations for moving vary, but here are five of the most common ones:

Cost of living. Many retirees are on a fixed income, and even if that's a comfortable one, who wants to pay high property taxes for a school district their kids no longer attend? Stretching your budget during retirement, so you can spend your hard-earned dollars on enjoying life, is a top reason why people move out of state when they downsize. And they look for states with lower taxes, affordable houses, manageable healthcare costs, and proximity to reputable healthcare facilities. (Hint: Read on to find out which of the top states and countries are attracting more and more empty nesters!)

Weather. Harsh winters and hot summers are strong deterrents. Many people look for more temperate climates in their golden years so they can shovel snow less and spend more time outdoors.

Family. Relocating to be closer to family is a top reason for moving. For more about what that entails, see chapters 3 and 4!

Tax benefits. While you think about the quality-of-life improvements moving might offer, consider the state tax breaks you may enjoy in retirement. State tax laws vary and influence estate planning and inheritance taxes—all of which are primary considerations when moving.

A new adventure! Yes, you might consider moving because of health benefits—like a lower elevation being easier on conditions such as chronic obstructive pulmonary disease (COPD) or sleep apnea. But maybe you just miss the pizza in NYC or Chicago, the smell of the ocean on the east coast, the majestic evergreens of the northwest, the low humidity in the southwest, or the sunshine in Florida. Wherever your sense of adventure takes you, there are housing options waiting.

Moving Out of State

Once you've made the decision to move and it takes you out of state, it's time to put together an action plan.

First, take a look at your current home and everything in it. If you've lived there for many years, it might seem overwhelming to think about packing up and moving. This is a good time to consider what you really want to take; what you may want to give to family and friends; and what you want to sell or donate.

You should also take an inventory of what you have. One way to keep track is to create categories of items, such as furniture, appliances, clothes, personal mementos, rugs, window coverings, and kitchen items. Or you could simply organize by room.

Next, determine what you're taking and what you're leaving.

If you're leaving or giving away items, you may want to have a garage sale or donate them.

What if you don't have enough time to do this and need to move quickly? You might find yourself in this situation if you have a quick sale or other circumstances where you have to leave your current home and move faster than you thought. In this case, it's important to find a storage facility. Sizes and costs of facilities vary, so do your research and don't overspend for space you aren't using. Shipping container storage, such as that offered by companies like PODS, give you the flexibility to pack in stages: Phase 1 is to declutter for selling. Phase 2 is the eventual move but without making multiple drives back and forth to the storage unit. Putting your belongings in storage gives you flexibility as you move from your current home and travel out of state to find and purchase your new one.

Where to Stay, Who to Know

Once you've made the decision to move, where do you start?

- *Get a referral for an expert Realtor.* Reach out to your local real estate professional for a referral to a Realtor in the city you're considering moving to. This is critical. The last thing you want to do is pick someone out of a hat, and cross your fingers that they'll be your trusty guide during one of the biggest decisions you could make. In this case, who you know is *really* important. Your local Realtor will connect you to reputable professionals you will need in your new community to complete the moving process.
- *Immerse yourself temporarily.* Let's say you've decided to move to Charlotte, North

Carolina. You've heard it's a vibrant city with a flourishing tech sector. But that's what you've *heard*. You don't really know until you spend some time there. And unless you actually have, you won't know for sure that it's the community for you. Answer: Rent a furnished Airbnb and spend some time learning about the community you are planning to call home. Go to the local farmers markets and grocery stores. Drive around and talk to the residents. Are the facilities and shops you need there? Do you like the pace of life? Does it feel like home? Immerse yourself in the community before you commit.

- *Consult with your financial advisor.* Each state has different tax burdens. Every situation is different, so make sure you connect with your CPA or financial advisor to discuss which state is most tax advantageous for your situation.

Do states with no income tax mean living there will cost less?

States with no income tax may seem attractive. But do your research because it doesn't necessarily mean it will cost less to live there. Many states make up for the lost revenue with other taxes or by reducing infrastructure, healthcare, and education services.

You'll also want to look at which states tax pensions, 401(k) distributions, and Social Security benefits.

Review your plans with your financial advisor and look at the total tax burden by state. This will help give you an apples-to-apples (or oranges-to-oranges if you move to Florida) comparison of how the states stack up. There are many websites that do this for you—but be aware that information changes frequently based on the latest data.

As of this writing, here are the states with no income tax: Alaska, Florida, Nevada, New Hampshire, Tennessee, South Dakota, Texas, Washington, and Wyoming. And according to Kiplinger, Delaware is one of the top states for retirees because they have no sales tax, no death tax, and low property taxes. Colorado has the third lowest property taxes in the country, and no estate or inheritance taxes. State and local sales taxes, however, are higher than the average.

Bottom line: Not having a state income tax alone doesn't paint a complete picture. Look at total tax burden, services provided (or reduced), and consult with your financial advisor to find out what works best for your situation.

Out of the Country

More and more Americans are retiring abroad for many reasons. When you retire in the US, you may be close to family and familiar with customs and culture. It's an easier transition. But others are finding that the excitement of a new country—not to mention a new lifestyle supported by how much further their savings can go—is the right move at this stage of life.

Consider these three important factors in conjunction with moving abroad: your health, your finances, and your lifestyle.

The cost of living and healthcare in the US is very high compared to other countries. This alone gives many people a strong reason to consider moving out of the country in their golden years. But as with everything, it's important to consider all sides of the equation. What may be a wonderful place to visit may not feel or cost the same as a resident.

If you do decide to move abroad, give yourself a full year to prepare the paperwork and logistics because every country is different. If you are considering retiring abroad, here are some of the more popular international spots for ex-pats:

Panama for its mild tropical culture, updated infrastructure, and coastal towns.

Mexico for a new culture that's somewhat familiar with many thriving communities of ex-pats.

Costa Rica for its quaint rural towns and bustling cities on both the Caribbean and Pacific coasts.

Greece for its easy visa process and flat tax that's appealing for investors.

Portugal for its beautiful coastlines, low cost of living, and easy access to Europe. It's one of the most popular retirement destinations on the planet!

No matter where you move, retire, or start a new adventure, try before you commit. Spend time there. Get to know the locals. Match your lifestyle to the community. Do your research and above all else, check in with your financial advisor.

Then, and only then, should you get a move on— literally!

And now, it's time to move on to chapter 6.

SIX

GET REAL ABOUT A REALTOR

"My wife and I have bought and sold many homes in our loving marriage. But the selling of our home in Conifer was the BEST EXPERI-ENCE! Jackie White was a dream to work with. Her level of professionalism is unmatched. I texted and called her at all hours of the day, and she always responded promptly. Even when we were met with challenges, Jackie always helped us keep our morale up and figured out a quick solution. She guaranteed us top dollar for the current market, and she GOT IT! If you're selling or buying a home and you don't use Jackie White, you're a fool."

"We had a very positive experience working with Jackie. She is a great communicator, knows her stuff, and gets it done efficiently. Jackie was very easy and pleasant to work with, always meeting our schedule and needs. We're deaf and she did not hesitate in providing an ASL interpreter for all of our important meetings. Would recommend!"

~

"Jackie was amazing! Prior to listing, she completed a very thorough assessment of our home and its market value. She presented her research to us and provided us with a fifty-plus-page market analysis. Our home sold in two days for full price with minimal concessions! Throughout the contract time period, Jackie was on top of all of the dates and deadlines and kept us up to date on everything (including the buyer's loan status and inspection). She was very responsive to our phone calls, emails, and texts, and she promptly and accurately answered any questions we had. She referred us to great service professionals (HVAC, roofing, and moving labor). I highly recommend using Jackie to sell your home. You won't be disappointed."

∼

Full disclosure: The above reviews are directly from Zillow and Realtor.com. I never offer anything in return for good reviews because my track record and work speaks for itself. And in the real estate industry, your reputation is the only sales tool you'll ever need.

So why am I sharing this?

Because as much as you might think it will be easier or more affordable to sell or buy your home on your own, you could be losing tens of thousands of dollars—or more—without having the data and information you need.

That's why finding the right Realtor is one of the most important things you can do when looking to downsize.

Here's what an experienced Realtor will do for you:

Analyze current market conditions. Think about the market fluctuations in your retirement fund. Do you trust yourself to time the market and ride the wave or surf the lows? A Realtor will be able to help you understand supply and demand fluctuations, economic factors, mortgage interest rate trends—and what all that means for you and your specific situation. In marketing, data is king. And good

Realtors have access to the data you need to tell you what the current market conditions mean for you—down to a very specific, hyper-localized level. Maybe you've heard "it's a seller's market" or "it's a buyer's market." Is that true? Is it true for you? And what does that mean? Market conditions can dictate home prices nearly as much as the neighborhood, age of the home, and so much more.

Get a Comparative Market Analysis (CMA). Let's face it—many people are emotionally attached to their homes. Maybe even you. We tend to overvalue the things we're attached to. Perhaps you look at your four-bedroom home and don't see that the massive remodel you did ten years ago is now considered outdated. It's a harsh truth, but *you* don't dictate what your house is going to sell for. The market does.

So where does your property rate? That's where a comparative market analysis comes into play. Your Realtor will share what houses in your neighborhood are selling for, recent comparable sales, and a lot more. This all helps you set a realistic and competitive price for your home so your property isn't sitting on the market forever —and so you're getting the fair value for your

property on your block and in your neighborhood.

Consider this: A 1,200 square foot apartment
in New York City might go for $2 million.
That same-sized apartment in Tulsa, Okla-
homa, could be $150,000. Location is part of
why you must get a comparative market
analysis—which a licensed Realtor is trained
to do.

Know Your Profit

The price of a home for sale is not what the seller pock-
ets. There are many other fees that come out of the sale
price. So where does that leave your profit and what
does that mean for how much you'll have for your next
purchase?

Mark and Rose are ready to downsize. They love
their large home, which they have owned for thirty-five
years, but the kids have all grown and have families of
their own. The grandkids are busy, so Mark and Rose
don't need all that space anymore. But they want a
modern condo that is easy to maintain—and has
enough extra bedrooms in case the grandkids want to
stay over.

Mark and Rose decide to sell their home but don't
know how much they will truly have in profit—which

will dictate how much they can then spend on their new modern condo. They hire an experienced Realtor who determines, based on a comparative market analysis and other data, that they should price their home at $825,000.

What will their profit be?

They bought their home thirty-five years ago for $175,000.

Their profit before costs and fees would be $650,000. (Nice to dream, right?) Some of the costs they're facing, which come out of the sale of their home, will include:

- Investment to sell the home, including staging costs, painting, and other repairs
- Title insurance and attorney's fees to close the transaction
- Realtor's commission
- Repairs required based on the buyer's home inspection

Let's assume that all those costs add up to $75,000. That means Mark and Rose have a profit of $575,000 on the sale of their home.

The condo they want to purchase is $600,000. This

THE UPSIDES TO DOWNSIZING

leaves them $25,000 needed to purchase their condo *after* they sell their home.

But wait! There's more!

Now Mark and Rose have to consider capital gains taxes on the sale of their home. And if they purchase their condo before they sell their home, they will have carrying costs on their home. See how complicated it can be? That's why knowledge is power! The costs add up and the ins and outs of real estate transactions can be complex. A good Realtor will break down all the numbers for you so that you are armed with information and knowledge to help you make the best decisions possible. You'll reduce uncertainty (and anxiety!) and avoid the common pitfalls many prospective home sellers and buyers can fall into without their trusty Realtor by their side.

Finding a Trusted Realtor

Trust is everything when it comes to finding the right Realtor. Realtors don't get paid until you sell or purchase your home, so you may think their interest is in putting a deal together quickly.

If you ever feel rushed, sound the alarm bells, raise the flags, and pull back. You should not feel rushed into making any decision you are not completely comfortable with.

Let me repeat that once more: Don't let anyone rush you into a decision you aren't comfortable with.

If you need a place to start, think about the people in your life whose opinions you trust. Your family, friends, or coworkers. Word of mouth is everything. Get recommendations from those closest to you. It could be someone you trust has used a Realtor personally or heard good things about one.

Is the Realtor who helped you buy your current property still working? Go back to who you know. Some prospective home buyers use word of mouth via signage in their neighborhood. Very often, a Realtor will have many homes they have sold in a particular neighborhood, and many will view them as the resident expert.

In this digital age, you should also look at reviews on Zillow.com, Google, or Realtor.com. Do your research! There are even neighborhood apps like Next-Door.com where you can post questions asking for recommendations for a Realtor.

Once you find some candidates you are interested in, make sure you check out their websites. Most will have their own websites or a page on a real estate agency's site. It's a good place to start to get to know them and their working style.

PRO TIP: Only consider someone who is licensed in your state so that you are confident they have met the minimum levels of education, training, and testing. Find out what trade associations they belong to, such as the National Association of Realtors, or whether they have special credentials like a SRES (Senior Real Estate Specialist).

Once you find your top candidates, the next step is setting up an appointment so they can see your home (if you're selling) or talk to you about what you're interested in buying. Give yourself at least an hour to show them your property and ask questions.

About those questions . . .

You should ask as many questions as you need to. It's important you feel comfortable before moving forward. You want someone who is going to be responsive and represent *your* interests not just theirs. Here are some of the most common questions to ask before you decide who should be your Realtor:

- What is your training and years of experience?
- How many homes have you sold and in what time period?
- Do you have a specific approach on how to price a home?
- How familiar are you with this neighborhood?
- What is your communication style?

- Do you develop a marketing plan to sell a home and what does that look like? Do you have an example?
- Now that you've seen our home, what repairs and preparation, if any, do you think need to be done to get it ready to put it on the market?
- What hours are you available to take calls or texts?
- What is your fee structure?
- Do you have references from recent home sales or purchases?

This is your chance to interview a potential agent. It's important you find the right Realtor for *you* and your needs—someone you can trust who will have your back and make sure the selling or buying process is seamless and successful.

After all, knowledge is one of the most valuable things you can have in *any* market. Make sure you've got as much of it as you can.

SEVEN

THE DOWN LOW ON DECLUTTERING

E ver heard the expression that one man's trash is another man's treasure? It's an expression that may have roots in the eighteenth century. But today, it has a different meaning when it comes to selling a home. Buyers may view one man's trash as simply . . . trash. That collection of sneakers in the basement? Or the guest room filled with souvenir spoons from every country? Those were likely once a source of pride for the homeowner—their treasures.

Buyers don't want to see spoon collections or the basement that has been decorated to look exactly like the locker room of your city's NFL team.

They want to picture themselves and *their* stuff in the house they are (hopefully) buying. And they can't do that very well (or at all) unless they, too, collect spoons and sneakers and love NFL team locker rooms.

Properly Preparing Your Home Is Critical

It takes a lot more effort than most people think to properly prepare a home for selling. Sure, there are things like spackling small holes in the wall. Or painting the room that has your grandchild's latest crayon portrait on the wall. Of course, you'll want to make sure the small details are attended to—like ensuring the lights have functioning bulbs and the faucets don't leak. (We'll talk about small repairs and bigger renovations in the next chapter!)

One of the most important things you can do to prepare your house to be on the market is to *declutter*.

Decluttering is more than throwing out stacks of papers, old bills, and the collection of empty soda cans. It is about creating an open and organized home that anyone could see themselves living in.

The family heirlooms on the credenza, the fridge covered in photos, the half-chewed pet toys strewn across the floor, they all should be put away.

Even a small number of personal items can be distracting for potential buyers. As much as it may pain you to store your treasured belongings, your job is to be a seller—to make the house looks as move-in ready as possible. You have to roll out the red carpet (in your just-cleaned foyer) and announce to buyers, "I bet you can see yourself living here and calling this your home."

To do that, here's the down low on decluttering.

Why Declutter?

Buyers will be more drawn to a space that is clean, organized, and well-maintained. Clutter makes your home appear smaller—and makes it harder for buyers to start visualizing where their own furniture and belongings would go. A neutral, clean slate is best and appeals to a variety of tastes.

You might look around your home and think, "Where do I start?" It may have taken you decades to fill the home with everything you have. How and where do you start to declutter without getting overwhelmed?

PRO TIP: Focus on one room at a time. Identify the rooms that either need the most attention or will get the most attention—like the living room or kitchen. Remember—first impressions count for a lot! You don't want a buyer to walk into your living room and be stopped cold by the plastic on the couches and the three-foot-high stack of magazines.

As you set your focus room by room, also consider narrowing in on one task at a time. For example, start small with a closet or set of drawers so you can "toss the trash"—not just obvious garbage but things you no longer need: broken toys, old remote controls, and duplicates of things that are just taking up space and making your home look disorganized and cluttered.

Create a plan

As you take inventory of each room, consider what you want to keep, what you want to toss, what you want to give away, and what you want to donate. Then get to work! Start organizing everything using bins, containers, and racks. Label your containers so you know what is where. Take photos on your phone to catalog everything, so when you're ready to sell, donate, or unpack your items, you know exactly which container holds which items.

Pare down the furniture

Furniture is necessary but too much takes up valuable space and makes rooms look small and cramped. Evaluate each piece of furniture and categorize by "nice to have" versus "need to have." For example, your couch is probably something you need to have but the neon clock on the wall from the 1950s diner is not. Keep the flow of space open and easy to navigate. Buyers are walking around your house. Make it easy for them!

This Isn't Personal

Selling your home may feel very personal to you, but buyers don't look at it through your lens. They look at it through *theirs*. All those wonderful family photos you have on end tables and desks and walls make you smile. And they still can—*once you sell your home and find a new place for them.* But if you want a buyer to make an offer, it's time to take all the personal photos off the wall and replace them with simple artwork or mirrors.

Clear the Decks!

Seriously, clear the decks. If you have a deck, put any kids' toys away and make sure the patio furniture is clean. If it needs a power wash, invest in one. And it's important to clear other surfaces and areas of your home: countertops, coffee tables, shelves. Leave only a few generic items out. Look at every level surface in your home and keep 80 percent of it free from clutter.

Don't forget to unstuff the closets because closet space is always a selling point. Make it feel open and large by putting away off-season clothes and organizing blouses, skirts, suits and pants by color, so they are hanging neatly.

Consider renting a storage unit for your items and furniture while you put your house on the market. The goal is not to have your home look sparse but to have it feel airy, open, and inviting.

And remember, there are professional organizers and junk removers who offer services to help you. Your Realtor should have a list and recommendations to make decluttering your home as easy on you as possible.

A Room-By-Room Guide to Decluttering

At the beginning of the chapter, I mentioned breaking down the task of decluttering room by room.

Here are more specifics for each room beyond the normal cleaning and dusting. Keep this checklist handy, and cross off items as you go!

Living Room

- Remove excess furniture
- Clear off coffee tables
- Remove photos and personal items
- Replace or clean worn furniture and rugs
- Ensure all light fixtures are working properly

Kitchen

- Clear countertops completely

- Organize cabinets and drawers
- Clean appliances inside and out
- Empty and clean the refrigerator inside and out
- Ensure all appliances are working properly

Bedrooms and Home Office

- Clear off nightstands and dressers
- Make the bed with clean, neutral bedding
- Organize closets and create a sense of ample storage space
- Make sure doors and light fixtures are working properly
- Stack papers and books neatly
- Empty trash cans

Bathrooms

- Clear countertops
- Scrub and re-caulk
- Replace rugs and shower curtains
- Ensure plumbing and faucets are working
- Make sure the medicine cabinet is organized
- Hang up clean towels
- Empty trashcans

Hallways, Entryways, and Garage

- Clear all clutter
- Ensure proper lighting
- Keep items in storage containers
- Remove excess coats and shoes
- Neatly store tools

PRO TIP: Don't neglect the front door. It'll be the buyer's first impression. Hang a welcome sign, apply a fresh coat of paint, and add a new welcome mat and a potted plant or flowers to your entryway.

Remember, decluttering creates an open, inviting space. You'll want to prepare your home for sale by cleaning, organizing, and creating a neutral environment. Once you do that, all that's left is to add the finishing touches: scented candles, fresh flowers, freshly baked cookies, and strategically placed mirrors.

If you prepare and declutter your home properly, all you have left to do is sit back and wait for the offers to start rolling in—unless your home needs some additional renovations. For more on that, read on!

EIGHT

SETTING THE STAGE FOR THE SALE

Susan's adult daughter, Rachel, and her husband were busy growing their family and managing the day-to-day logistics of four kids under the age of ten. Susan knew it was hard for Rachel and the kids to find time to travel to see her, and she wanted to be closer to help with her four grandkids. Susan was excited about this new chapter in her life and used it as an excuse to reduce the belongings she had collected over the years.

If she had to move into an assisted housing facility unexpectedly, it would have been a burden on Rachel to have to sort through Susan's belongings. Rachel and her brother's style didn't quite match Susan's love of antiques, and they would have felt guilty donating mom's cherished collections.

Susan sold or donated items she no longer needed, and kept a few possessions she still enjoyed, like a couple colorful vases and artwork to decorate her new home. Susan was able to make some money on the sale of her belongings and knew someone else would enjoy them, and she wasn't paying to move these items that would not fit in her new patio home!

~

Like Susan, maybe you've lived in your home for years. You think it looks great. You took down the old wallpaper and painted. Your stove is ten years old, but it's working just fine.

When you list your home for sale, a potential buyer is viewing your home through a much different lens. What's new to you might be old news to them.

If you're thinking about putting your house on the market, you face a decision either to make updates for a future sale or price your home now for current market conditions.

Regardless of which you choose, the very first thing you should do is consult with your Realtor. You don't want to take on projects that cost a lot but will have little impact on your sale price. Your Realtor also will be able to advise you on whether what you update, considering market conditions, is really worth the cost. And they can tell you if the renovations you are planning will take enough time that it could push you out of the optimal seasonal window to sell your home.

To get your house ready for a sale, start small. At a minimum fix the little annoyances you may have lived with—door handles that are loose, a small hole in the wall, the leaky faucet. These must be repaired to get your house ready for sale.

More extensive renovations require planning and budgeting. But the investment might be well worth it because the goal is to make your home as attractive to buyers as possible to sell it faster and for a higher price.

So, which should you do—small repairs or major renovations? Read on.

Is your home a victim of deferred maintenance?

Deferred maintenance is a fancy way of saying that you kicked the can down the road on some needed home repairs—and all those little issues have now accumulated over time. The rusty pipe or the loose floorboard—or any number of needed repairs—can add up like compound interest and deter potential buyers.

Some sellers think that they will find a buyer who is willing to take the house as is. Don't bet on it. Although those buyers are out there, most don't want to take on projects. They want to purchase a house that is move-in ready, so they can walk in and start enjoying it.

Repair Basics

The "No-Brainer" Fixes

There are, of course, some investments in your home that you can make that will no doubt help improve your home's value without incurring a hefty amount of time or costs. These include:

- Wall repairs to cover nail holes
- Fresh paint in neutral colors
- New carpet in neutral colors
- New paint on cabinets
- Repairing appliances

Moving Up the Cost Ladder

- Updating countertops
- Replacing appliances
- Deck repairs
- New garage door
- Replacing windows and doors

Major Renovations

When it comes to major renovations, you've no doubt heard that bathrooms and kitchens are where to focus because they provide a better return on your investment. And though these big projects may seem like a daunting task, the results can dramatically increase the price you get for your home versus selling it in the condition it is now.

Think about it—how many times have you looked at your kitchen and bathroom and thought about gutting it and starting over? Most of us have. What stops us? Money and time. But if you have both before you sell, the investment can be worth the reward.

PRO TIP: With any home improvement project, proceed with caution. Often contractors tackling major renovations discover other issues along the way. Hidden problems behind walls, in attics, or under roofs. Suddenly, the kitchen redo now involves a major plumbing overhaul—and a major new expense.

On the plus side, you might discover some pleasant surprises. If you have an older home, you might find that pulling up the carpet reveals beautiful hardwood that's in good shape and just needs some refinishing. Anyone who has taken on major home improvements knows to expect the unexpected—good and bad.

Be sure to consult your Realtor before taking on any major renovations to decide if the costs to your pocketbook (and your sanity) are worth it.

Who Is Your Buyer?

Here's a simple answer: *you* are not your buyer. In marketing one of the first rules is to know your audience. Well, your audience is the buyer!

The odds are very good that your buyer may be part of the millennial generation—such as younger families. And consider this: on average, sellers over the age of fifty-four have lived in their homes for twelve to seventeen years before putting it on the market. Times and design tastes change more quickly than you think! Remember the avocado color appliances in the 1960s and 1970s? Millennials may not think your home is updated at all—even though it can seem like you just remodeled it.

And here's something else: Many younger buyers don't want to put time or money into renovations. They're busy with jobs and kids and may only want a home that is move-in ready. The data supports this: 2019 NAR Home Buyer and Seller Generational Trends reports percentage of buyers by age who purchased a new home to "avoid renovations or problems with plumbing or electricity."

28 and younger	29–38	39–53	54–63	64–72	73–93
74%	51%	39%	30%	27%	29%

Your Local Market

Finally, a word on your local market. Every market is unique. Trends and data across the country can vary quite a bit. That's why consulting with a Realtor is so important.

And if you're over fifty, you might benefit from a Senior Real Estate Specialist who understands today's generational differences between buyers and sellers.

All the World's a Stage

Imagine walking into a home for sale, and you're hit with a musty smell from the basement, and you see shag carpeting and outdated wallpaper. First impressions count.

Now imagine you walk into warm, soft colors, comfortable furniture, and the smell of freshly baked chocolate chip cookies.

Which feels more like home to you?

That's the power of staging!

Whether you decide to do minor repairs or renovate, you should always consider staging your home to make it more attractive to buyers. Staging provides a perception so buyers can envision themselves living in your home. The goal is to create an inviting atmosphere.

Staging Strategies to Consider

The first staging strategy is to depersonalize your home. Remember that this is a business transaction at the end of the day. You want to remove from your home any personal items you own so buyers see a clean slate for themselves. Think of it like a blank canvas. That means putting away family photos lining the credenza and your collection of jade monkeys from the Far East. Remember Susan from the beginning of this chapter? Because she had already reduced the number of personal belongings in her home, it was easier to stage her home for sale.

Next, clean and declutter. We've talked about decluttering and cleaning many times thus far, but we can't stress it enough. It is a critical step to getting your home ready for sale. Deep clean every room—baseboards, windowsills, fixtures, ceiling fans, vents, and more. Clear surfaces to make your home feel larger and more open.

When it comes to your furniture, the art of the arrangement can be crucial. Remove excess furniture (large bean bag, anyone?) to make the home flow better. A person who is a professional stager can offer you invaluable ideas.

You will also want to stage your home to include neutral tones—soft grays and whites, for example. Neutral tones are versatile and help convey that blank slate buyers want.

PRO TIP: Here's a quick and easy way to make your home brighter. Update your lighting so that your home is well-lit through a combination of natural and artificial lighting. Replace outdated light fixtures and open curtains and blinds to let the natural light in

Still on the fence about staging your home?

- Studies show that staged homes sell up to 79 percent faster than vacant homes.
- According to the National Association of Realtors, 81 percent of agents representing buyers said staging a home made it easier for a buyer to visualize the property as a future home.
- If the housing market is sluggish, staging will give your home an attractive edge over the competition.

Whether you repair or renovate, hire a professional

stager or do it yourself, remember that a move-in ready home will likely sell for more and sell faster.

The time, planning, and money you invest now could yield higher rewards down the road.

So, grab a cup of coffee and prepare for an in-depth discussion with your Realtor about what it will take to get your home ready to put on the market.

Then sit back and watch the offers roll in!

NINE

IT'S ALL ABOUT TIMING

Stan and Donna moved to their small mountain town in the early 1970s when it was a sleepy little community. They built a house themselves and raised their two sons in the home while making countless friends along the way.

As the community became more popular over the years, home prices and values increased significantly, and the quiet town grew around them. The value of their home increased tenfold since they purchased it! But so did the tax assessment and homeowners' insurance on what was now a quite valuable home.

They found themselves in a position of being house rich and cash poor as they did not anticipate the rapid rise of cost of homeownership as retirees. Stan and Donna decided they were ready to downsize and capture the equity in their home to use in retirement.

They downsized to a townhome that was less than twenty minutes from their former home, which was close enough to continue to socialize with their lifelong friends. They both are quite active. Stan is a pickleball player and Donna is an avid golfer, so making friends in their new town was easy!

The newfound cash reserves from the sale of their old home eased their financial stress, and Donna is looking forward to taking a trip to visit her sisters in Maryland a few more times a year.

❧

Stan and Donna made an investment that grew over time. And timing was on their side again as they used the equity in their home for retirement. They made a wise decision and benefitted from optimal timing.

In fact, most things in life come down to timing, and selling or buying a home is no different. Perhaps you're ready to sell now, but the market conditions favor buyers not sellers. Or maybe you have time to wait, so you decide to sit on your house until market conditions are better. But that could also mean you wait ... and wait ... and wait.

Unless you're incredibly lucky, you'll probably find

yourself needing to sell or buy a home when market conditions are not as optimal as they could be. That's where your trusty, reliable Realtor who can evaluate the market for you and remove the guesswork comes in. Your Realtor, who knows historical trends in the market and can help you make an informed decision, is looking out for your best interests, so you don't have to wade into a housing market blindly.

Have we made it clear you should really connect with a reputable Realtor? Those are steps 1, 2, and 3 of the downsizing process.

Here are some other key factors to consider when timing the sale of your home and the purchase of another.

Seasonality

Seasonality sounds like it could be about how spicy you like your food. But in this case, it refers to market conditions in a specific area. There are ebbs and flows in how quickly houses sell based on the school year, season, and other factors. Some seasons are more favorable for selling and others for buying. Check with (wait for it…) your Realtor for the specific seasonality trends in your area.

Personal Commitments

If you have any personal events that will require your time and attention, make sure to communicate it to your Realtor. Do you have a wedding or an anniversary trip planned? Is there a grandchild on the way that might take you across the country for a while? Or perhaps you or a loved one have a health issue, and you might need to spend a good chunk of your time at medical appointments. No matter the commitment, communicate your schedule and priorities to your Realtor, so they can time the sale of your home when it works with the market and is best for you.

Selling Before Winter

Winter can be the toughest time to sell a home. But it can also work in your favor with fewer homes on the market. Fewer homes on the market means fewer options for buyers, and less competition for your home. Plus, if a buyer is willing to brave the cold and snow to look for a new home, they are probably pretty motivated. You may have fewer buyers visiting your home, but the ones who do come probably are not simply browsing. Talk to your Realtor about the pros and cons of getting your house ready for sale before winter hits and if you have enough lead time to make it happen.

You've Sold Your Home—Now What?

Let's say you've timed the market well. You've decluttered, made repairs, and staged your home.

And your house sells quickly. Congratulations!

The amount of time and energy you would have spent with your home continuing to be on the market can now be channeled into your next chapter.

But where do you live if your house sells quickly? This is a common scenario and there are many options for you like living with friends or family or in short-term rentals.

If your house doesn't sell quickly and you start looking at new homes, make sure you can afford to buy before you sell your current one. If you can, then pop the champagne and pack up your boxes!

If you need the equity from your house to purchase your new one, market conditions will dictate if you can make your offer contingent on the sale of your current home. Many sellers may pass on your offer because waiting for your current home to sell is an unknown, which poses a risk to them. If they say yes to you and then have to wait for your home to sell, they could be waiting for a very long time. And so could you because if the market is favorable for sellers, they will probably have other offers with no contingencies at all.

If you do sell your home before you have a new one, one option is to negotiate a leaseback deal with your buyer where you stay in the home for a few weeks to a few months after the sale, so you have additional time to find your new home.

Bottom line: There are places to live if your house sells quickly. You won't be homeless! Let your Realtor walk you through the process and options.

Prepare for a Rental

Unless you have very generous family and friends who will allow you to move in for a while, you should assume you will have to live in a rental of some sort in between the sale of your current home and the purchase of a new one. Short-term rentals through services like Airbnb and VRBO can give you furnished, easy solutions for a few weeks to a few months.

Ready to evaluate the timing of putting your house on the market? Here are some questions to ask your Realtor:

- When historically is the best time to sell?
- What are market conditions like right now?
- If I need to sell before the winter, when should I put my house on the market?
- I have some personal events coming up. Should I wait to put my house on the market?

- How do I time the sale of my home and the purchase of a new one?
- If I need the equity in my current home to buy a new one, how do we time that?
- If my house sells quickly, can I negotiate staying in my home for a few weeks?
- If my house doesn't sell quickly, what can we do to make it more attractive to buyers?
- Should I time the market or prepare to put my house up for sale no matter what?

Remember, knowledge is power.

And while nobody can time the market perfectly, being informed gives you control over your decisions and can help you navigate the complexities and timing of an effective and profitable home sale.

But so can your Realtor. Choose one wisely!

TEN

GO FORTH AND DOWNSIZE!

Nancy and Ed owned a modest-sized ranch-style home on two acres in a popular neighborhood. They raised their daughter in the home, and a horse as well! The home wasn't difficult to maintain due to its size, but Nancy and Ed quickly found themselves with health issues they were not expecting. This limited their mobility and energy, often leaving them tired after doing only a few simple household chores.

Caring for the property quickly became too much to handle. Nancy researched living options where they could get a little extra help when needed and found an independent living community. The single level home was similar to what they currently had, but their monthly housing fee also included maintenance inside and out plus weekly housekeeping. This help allowed Nancy and Ed not to tire from their chores and still have the energy to partici-pate in a few of the social activities, organized outings, and local tours coordinated by the activity director.

The new home is allowing Nancy and Ed to live stress-free while maintaining their independence!

~

Take it from Nancy and Ed. They knew the time was right to downsize—and downsize they did. In the process, they upsized their lifestyle and reduced their stress.

We all have different phases and chapters in our lives, and downsizing is no different. It's a natural evolution. But there are many complexities to consider as you downsize, as we've discussed throughout this guide. So, let's run through the big ones.

Are You Ready?

It seems like such a simple question, but you need to ask yourself and your family if you're truly ready for this next chapter. Moving to a new home or commu-nity should be an exciting step for you. You'll want to make sure you're 100 percent ready for this next phase of your life.

Don't Defer Decisions

Nobody knows what the future holds. If you're fully able to make decisions now, it puts *you* in control of your next home and living situation—versus further down the road when you may need family members to make decisions for you. That can be a burden on both them and you. Consider where you are in your life and move forward knowing *you* are dictating the terms not someone else.

Don't Be Nervous!

It's totally normal to be nervous about such a big life change, but you have so much to look forward to. The next chapter of your life should bring you excitement and joy!

Hire a Great Realtor

Think of your Realtor as your trusty guide, navigating the complexities and every step of the way. That's why you should take great care hiring a Realtor—who you click with—who answers your questions patiently, and who knows your market and has the experience to help you sell your home and/or buy your next one.

Your Realtor will:

- Set realistic expectations about what your house could sell for and how long it might be on the market.
- Provide you with a list of professionals in your area for everything from home inspections to staging.
- Develop a strategic and tailored marketing plan to attract buyers and help your house stand out from the competition.
- Skillfully negotiate on your behalf to get the best deal possible for you.
- Guide you through the closing process, including paperwork, and connecting you with everyone from inspectors to insurance agents.

Wrapping It All Up

So why downsize?

Perhaps the question is Why *not* downsize?

Why *not* free up your budget to do the things you enjoy?

Why *not* consider how your family fits into this new transition?

Why *not* plan for it while you can and are fully in control of your own decisions?

Why *not* find a new home that fits this next stage of your life?

Why *not* embrace this exciting new chapter with confidence?

In fact, why *not* start right now?

If you've read this guide from front to back, then you know exactly why you should start now, what to keep in mind, and who to start with: **a great Realtor.**

ABOUT THE AUTHOR

Jackie White is a licensed Realtor and real estate investor in the Denver, Colorado, area who has sold over three hundred homes in the past decade alone. She likes to say she knows the foothills of Denver like the back of her truck. Jackie specializes in helping families downsize when they're ready, walking them through the process and making the transition to the next chapter of their life and their homes as easy as possible. She is a Senior Real Estate Specialist, a Certified Negotiation Expert, and a Certified Mountain Area Specialist.

Known for her authentic, no-nonsense approach, Jackie consistently gets five-star reviews from her clients. When she's not helping people downsize to the home of their dreams for easy living, she is a volunteer at the fire department and can be seen driving her kids to their next sporting event with her trusted yellow lab, Platte, by her side.

"I highly recommend Jackie. She did an exceptional job for us in the sale of our home. I'll admit we considered going with one of the online discount agents. Boy, am I glad we didn't!! Jackie has a knowledge of the area that is difficult to match. She understood our home was more than the number of bedrooms, bathrooms, and square footage. The transaction was very easy, and Jackie kept us apprised the entire time. Thank you, Jackie!" —Link and Lisa S., Sold a home in the Morrison, CO foothills and moved to a home in the Denver suburbs

"We used Jackie to purchase our mountain home in Colorado. Jackie was fantastic! The market was competitive. Jackie went to each home we were interested in, discussed the pros and cons of each home with us, and outlined the best way to submit a winning bid. Once our bid was accepted, she gave us sound advice on how to close the deal. We saved a lot of money! My wife and I highly recommend Jackie." —Michael and Deb H., Purchased a second home to transition to Conifer, CO from Maryland

"Jackie is the absolute best in helping you buy or sell a home. She works tirelessly on your behalf and goes above and beyond in all aspects of your real estate transaction from initial contract to closing and all points in between. Jackie worked very closely with us on ensuring our builder was complying with terms of the contract and visited the new build frequently on our behalf to provide us updates on the status of the build. Jackie was always available for calls to answer questions or provide guidance on issues we encountered. Most importantly, she is a great person." —Sig and Pat A., Downsized from a home in Bailey, CO to a "lock and leave" townhome

AUTHOR'S CONTACT INFORMATION

Phone:
720-475-6111

Email:
jackiewhiterealtor@gmail.com

Website:
JackieWhiteRealtor.com

Facebook:
Fb.com/JackieWhiteRealtor

Read more reviews here:
https://www.zillow.com/profile/JackieWhiteDenver/
#reviews